Kindle Success Hacks
Business Realities and Insider Secrets
by
Tom Morgan
Literary Agent,Book Doctor and Publisher

Then shoot me a mail at **firstclass.artists@gmail.com** with "FREECON " in the subject line. We'll jump on skype/email and you can hit me with any and all self-publishing questions. Deal ?

On no !...not *another* ''How To Make A Million with Kindle '' Book !!!
No worries. This book is not about media fueled fantasies. It's about REALITY.

Specifically, three realities :

1. You're not going to make a million with Kindle. Consider yourself blessed if you make any money with self-publishing.
2. Self publishing is a business . Your book, regardless of how near and dear to your heart – is a *product.*
3. To sell that product – you need to be hip to the BUSINESS REALITIES of self-publishing. Particularly as they apply to Kindle.

As a Literary Agent, Book Doctor and Publisher, I know a thing or three about surfing these realities.

In this book, you'll learn these realities and how to apply them to OPTIMIZE your chances of Self-Publishing Success.

Just two more things :

1. If you're just "in it for the money " - leave this page NOW. This information is only for Authors who want to provide VALUE.

2. If you're not willing to invest a minimum of $500 in your career to implement these nuggets – you're wasting your time here. It really does "take money to make money. " (Yes, more reality!)

Still with me ? – OK , let's dive in !

Introduction

Oscar Wilde once said (or at least is reputed to have said) " Success is a Science . If you have the ingredients – you get the results." I agree with that 99%. Because in self publishing, as in any commerical Artistic endeavor – there will be 1% who are "Struck by lightning. " Amanda Hocking being the classic example. She did nothing but upload her book to Kindle, and readers rushed in like shoppers on a free hour.

Even She is unable to explain it. "I've looked at other books in the same genre as mine, and they're well written, and selling ok....but nowhere near as much as mine."

Think you could be another Amanda Hocking ? Totally possible. But also Totally improbable. Like to stake your career on it ? (Didn't think so)

Every Artistic creation is unequal parts inspiration and craft. You were inspired to write your book, to share your message. You had the craft, the knowledge of language, the determination to turn that inspiration into a shareable form.

Now – you need to get eyeballs on that shareable form.

Before we get started – there will be some information you already know – or more accurately *think* you know. Don't assume. Don't skim. Do yourself a favor and read everything. It's Short. But powerful.

OK – let's Roll !

Chapter One

The Nature of the Beast

Before we – ''get to the gold'' is important to clearly understand Amazon and it's objectives.

Amazon, simply put, wants to completely dominate internet commerce. What ? You mean it isn't already ? Not yet....but it's on the way there. Everything Amazon does (whether obvious or not) is focused on this goal.

Books ,you'll probably be surprised to learn, aren't a big part of Azon's domination plan. They were/are just one of many strategies to increase their user base and gather credit cards.

Which means, bottom line , if/when ''The Big A '' decides that books aren't ''pulling their weight'', they won't hesitate to axe them. Or downgrade their features. From the Authors side . They would NEVER do anything to upset a customer.

And that is your great advantage as an Author. Because Azon, as it proudly (and repeatedly) proclaims is : ''The World's most customer-centric company''

If you, the Author are pleasing those customers, Mr. Bezos and Co. Are going to reward you by promoting your book, for free, to those customers.

That, for Authors is the true ''Amazon Advantage ''

Chapter Two

What's in a Name ?

There is a three step Sequence that gets a surfers eyeballs on your book : Title. Cover. Description. Miss any one, and those eyeballs(and that potential sale) go elsewhere.

Basic One : Title.

The second most important essential. It needs to be *Fantastic !*

How do you come up with a fantastic title ? First, and most obvious, you check out the titles in your genre that appeal to you. Note them. Then, check out the "customers who bought this book also bought " section at the bottom of the listing page. Note them also.

Next, using the Azon titles you collected, and whatever brillant original titles you've managed to brainstorm, you play mix n' match with the assembled multitude.

When you have a shortlist of the possible "candidates", you 'phone friends and just read two choices at a time.(Assuming you have more than two) You'll get an instant, honest answer. Because it's a telephone exchange where the possibility of additional face to face discussion doesn't exist. THAT'S why Mr. Bell's swell invention is best.

If you get stuck – try plays on words, double entendres, using familiar sayings/expressions. Anything, however dumb it seems, to get the creative juices flowing.

HOT TIP : *When one of my Authors does this, he records everything, because, as you will find, usually the ideas and variations come too fast to write down.*

Before I give you some examples of Fantastic Titles , keep in mind, that creativity is more important than keywords.

Naturally, the best of both worlds is a Fantastic Title that includes both.

The ever popular "How To" Titles :

How to Increase your Productivity
How to Get Your Point Across in 30 Seconds or less
How to Avoid Falling in Love with a Jerk

Ok – all pretty straightforward titles – what you see is what you get .

This next title - How to Get Your ex Back Fast- is also, direct. But, by itself, not very captivating...until the Author (wisely) adds this subtitle : *toy with the male psyche and get him back with skills only a dating coach knows*

Instantly this sub head tells you (a) this book is for women and (b) it creates a desire to know how to "toy with the male psyche."

Here are two other examples of sub-titles – "bringing home the bacon"

Goals Suck : Why the Obsession with Goal-setting is a Flawed Approach to Productivity and life in General

Book Marketing is Dead : book promotion secrets you MUST know BEFORE you publish your book.

Humor continues to be one of the most effective ways to get attention. As these titles confirm :

The Earth, My Butt, and Other Big Round Things
Cloudy With a Chance of Meatballs
When will Jesus Bring the Pork Chops ?

Mystical/Reflective Titles arouse our curiosity :

The Unbearable Lightness of Being
Midnight in the Garden of Good and Evil
The Songs of Distant Earth

Likewise for **Titles that are ambiguous** and/or weird :

Do Androids Dream of Electric Sheep?
Snakes on a Plane.
The Hollow Chocolate Bunnies of the Apocalypse.

Contrarian Titles can also be very effective attention getters :

I Have No Mouth – But I must Scream - being one of my favs !

Or a contrarian take on a popular classic :

How to Lose Friends and Alienate People

Shock Titles are another guaranteed attention getter :

Don't Pee on My Leg and Tell Me It's Raining: America's Toughest Family Court Judge Speaks Out
How to Shit in the Woods: An Environmentally Sound Approach to a Lost Art
Go the Fuck to Sleep

But, keep in mind if you go this route, shock titles always must follow through with a

<u>qualifying sub-title.</u> As the first two above do.

Did you notice - All of those Titles, regardless of whether they're Fiction or Non-Fiction have one thing in common ? : <u>CREATIVITY</u>. Which is not necessarily "Originality."

<u>Innovation</u>, as you've just seen from my examples,<u> is a classic example of creativity.</u>

The second Creative element you saw in all 90% of those titles was ??? - yes, you're right again ! - <u>CURIOSITY</u> ! It may have "killed the cat" – but it is (with the exception of humorous titles) the "lifeblood" of a fantastic book title.

Chapter Three

<u>C</u>overing <u>Y</u>our <u>B</u>utt

Basic **T**wo : <u>Cover.</u> The first most important essential. It needs to be *Phenomenal !!!* Because you have only three short seconds to snag those eyeballs. Therefore – your convey must *instantly* convey the essence of your book.

The best route here, is the most obvious one. You scan all the covers in your genre . Which one(s) capture your instant attention. Why ? Image ? Color ? Graphics ? Fonts ? Layout ? All/some of the above ?

Copy the best into a folder . Study them until you understand what elements attract you and why. Use your knowledge to create some cover "mock ups." (Yes, it's cut n' paste time!)

HOT TIP : *<u>Because your cover needs to rock at a very small size, upload your mockup to your image creation software(photoshop/gimp,picmonkey,etc), download a kindle cover thumbnail, and reduce your mock up to the same size.</u>*

This will ensure you don't commit any image faux pas.

Generally speaking (which is always dangerous) a "good cover " is clean, uncluttered,no more than two colors, with arresting graphic design. And above all"pops" at thumbnail size !

Here are some examples :

 (Type the Title and /or Author in the Amazon search bar)

Breakthrough Your B.S. - *by Derek Doepker.*

And then She Was Gone – *by Christopher Grayson*

Enchantment – *by Guy Kawasaki*

The Ketogenic Diet – *by Wyatt Sullivan*

Success – *by Jaidyn Smith*

Basic **T**hree : **B**ook **De**scription

Assuming you've been skilled, talented, and/or lucky enough to entice the potential reader this far – you now have to, as succintly (and emotively) as possible, expand on the promise of your Title and Cover.

This is your last change to morph that surfer into a reader. So ''good'' – isn't going to cut it. Your description needs to be *riveting !*

Other than writing in the third person, your text should use action verbs appropriate to your genre, invoke curiosity, and set up a ''Cliffhanger '' scenario that will compel the reader to rush to your Kindle preview. (The first 10% of your book)

HOT TIP : *Don't shoot yourself in the foot by cluttering your book with 'front matter.'' (acknowledgements, thank you's, dedications, etc.) After title/author/copyright – get straight to what the reader came for. And make it your BEST Chapter.*

Here are some examples of riveting book descriptions :

First – A Fiction thriller...

''*Magazine journalist Seneca Hunt is reporting on the opening of Montezuma's tomb in Mexico City when the dig team learns that the remains of the Aztec emperor are* missing. *Within moments of the discovery, an apparent terrorist attack kills everyone at the site except Seneca, who barely escapes the carnage.*

Determined to get answers, Seneca starts investigating. She finds out that someone is stealing the remains of the most infamous mass murderers in history-and plotting to slaughter millions in the name of an ancient cult. Seneca needs to prove the threat really exists while trying to stay one step ahead of those who want her dead. With time running out, she must follow a deadly 2,000-year-old trail that leads back to the death of Jesus Christ."

Here the Author, by "giving away" the plot structure, is creating maximum curiosity. Virutally every sentence leaves the reader wondering "what will happen next ?" A classic example of a "cliffhanger" description.

This next description-a legal thriller, accomplishes the same goal. But without the terrorists, mass murderers and ancient Aztec remains :

"When sixteen-year-old Hannah Sheraton is arrested for the murder of her stepgrandfather, the chief justice of the California Supreme court, her distraught mother turns to her old college roommate, Josie Baylor-Bates, for help. Josie, once a

hot-shot criminal defense attorney, left the fast track behind for a small practice in Hermosa Beach, California. But Hannah Sheraton intrigues her and, when the girl is charged as an adult, Josie cannot turn her back. But the deeper she digs the more Josie realizes that politics, the law and family relationships create a combustible and dangerous situation. When the horrible truth is uncovered it can save Hannah Sheraton or destroy them both. "

This non-Fiction description, for a book critical of the Paleo Diet, takes a different approach to arousing curiosity. By injecting a heavy dose of fear. Fear of the possible consequences of following the Paleo Diet :

"Do you want to be ripped, lean, alert, full of natural energy? Totally "in tune" with your body and it's environment? Enjoying optimum health and vitality?

And to get all that, are you willing to risk:

Artery clogging saturated fats and bad cholesterol,(resulting in lower good cholesterol), bone-damaging acidic proteins, atheroslerosis, heart disease, protein toxicity(nausea, vomiting, diarrhea, and in extreme cases, death),type-2 diabetes, hypertension, hypercholesterolemia, arthritis, obesity, water retention,weight gain,fatigue plus vitamin and mineral deficiences?

A respected nutritionist (Himself a Paleo Author) reveals thats EXACTLY what you're risking with the uber-popular Paleo Diet.

You'll be shocked to learn that this diet, embraced by millions, is a ''stew'' of brief incomplete ''studies'', unproveable theories, misconceptions, assumptions , unverifiable projections, and massive self-promoting media hype.

If you believe '''you are what you eat'' - you need to chow down on this book.''

<u>Bottom Line</u> : By whatever means, in whatever genre, your book description needs to generate insatiable curiosity. Curosity that compels the surfer to '' buy with one click ! ''

Chapter Four

<u>E</u>nhanced <u>B</u>ook <u>D</u>escriptions

HACK ATTACK !

You've probably seen some book descriptions that have colored and /or bolded text. Emphasizing the major points(usually keywords!) the Author wants to stress.

And I'll bet you've wondered : ''How do they do that ?''

The answer is: HTML (hyper text markup language) the basic code that powers the majority of internet websites. Yes, it does look like Greek. Strange symbols.Squiggly lines. Bizzare jargon.

That's the bad news. The good news is that you don't need to be a tech geek to use a few simple html hacks to use color, bolding, strikethroughs and other graphic goodies in your riveting book description.

This site/link – http://tckpublishing.com/how-to-use-html-to-format-kdp-kindle-book-descriptions/ - explains it all.

But, be warned – no matter how careful and methodical you are – you WILL make mistakes. And you WILL cringe when you see your – let me be kind – less than perfect formatting live for all the World to see.

But – no worries. Because you can go in and try again until you get it right .(usually the second time)

However it will take 12 to 24 hours after you make the corrections until they're updated and live in the Kindle store.

Chapter Five

Basic **F**our : <u>Category</u>

Amazon allows you to select two categories for your book. While this seems to be a straightforward "no brainer" – ie – just select the two closest to your books genre - in reality - category selection is a very big can o' worms.

Because"The Big A" is constantly(meaning daily!) changing them(and even has some that aren't listed)Yes, it's the classic "Changing the rules in the middle of the game."

That's the bad news. The good news is that if you can place your book in one or ideally two "less populated" categories.....the book surfer has a better chance of finding yours. Specifically, (and ideally) you want to find high traffic/low competition categories.

You may have noticed that some books, on their sales page, are listed in more than two categories. And/or<u> in a category that is not listed.</u> (Literature and Fiction>Romance>Series, is one.)

You can usually finesse this by contacting Amazon and asking them to do your bidding.(Note : "usually " means it's a good "maybe" not a slam dunk .)

It's essential that you place your book in two different categories . Let's assume you have a French Travel book. The "logical" two categories would be :

Kindle Store>Kindle ebooks>Nonfiction>Travel>Europe>
Kindle Store>Kindle ebooks>Nonfiction>Travel>Europe>France

But "logical' isn 't effective here. By listing your book this way – you're shooting yourself in the foot. But if , for the second category you choose :

Kindle Store>Kindle eBooks>Humor>Entertainment>Humor>Essays

Now, other (non travel oriented) readers have a chance to find your book. Two chances are better than one. Right ?

But don't snooze once you've dialed in your categories. You need to keep checking them(at least every week) to make sure you don't get downgraded by Azon's upgrades.

Chapter Six

Basic Five : <u>Keywords.</u>

"Keywords" are those words and phrases that you type into your internet browser(or in this case the Azon search box) to find whatever you're looking for.

For example : if you're looking for a Romance book, "Romance" "Contemporary Romance", "Romance Erotica", "Romance book by my favorite author" are all words/phrase that are "key" to connecting to your desired content.

Amazon gives you seven keywords/phrases that(ideally) should help lead surfers to your magnum opus. Think of these as exactly what they are. Seven more (potential) chances for readers to find you.

So, obviously your choices have to be as totally "on the money" as possible.

Yes, it does sound like a daunting (and not much fun) task. And, truthfully it can be . Depending on your attitude. And yours is positive - right ?

But there is some good news. <u>Amazon has already done your research for you</u>.

Just like "Google Suggest" (the variations on what you type in the big G's search bar), you can(and absolutely should) do the same with your (imagined) perfect keywords in the Azon search window.

For example : Typing "Romance" returns : "Free Romance Books for Kindle", "Romance Novels", and " Free Romance Books" as the top three results. (Note : each time you type the same keyword/phrase – Azon will return slightly/very different results.

Although Mr. Bezos and Co. don't tell us *how* they arrive at the ORDER of the search results, it's logical to assume (given the fact that their default category is "relevance") that the first three are the most important.

So – Part One of finding your perfect keywords is typing your main keyword in the Azon search bar, followed by the letter "A." And noting the results. Then the letter "B." And so on. Until you've covered the entire alphabet.

Part Two goes like this : Check out the best selling books in the two categories you've chosen. Read their descriptions carefully, noting what obvious keywords they've used. Type those keywords into the search bar and see where they lead you. Should be to the book in question. Otherwise note where they do lead.

At the bottom of the book's sales page, check out the books that appear in the "also bought" category. (ie "customers who bought this book also bought.... ")
This will give you more "keyword intel."

They are some "Kindle gurus" who suggest typing your Azon acquired keywords/phrases into Google. And see what commonalities occur. WHY ?

The logic here escapes me. Readers search for books where books are sold. And for 60% of the book buying market – that's Amazon. (There is one exception here. Hang in, I'll explain it later.)

At the end of the day – you'll have a monster list of keywords to choose from. And that's the rock and the hard place. From all your meticulous, exhaustive, time consuming research, how do you choose the best seven keywords for you ?

The best (and honest) answer is : Just do your best. And don't sweat it. You can change your keywords(and categories) any time.

Bottom Line : After all your blood, sweat and tears, you're bound to get at least ONE out of seven right. And one is all it takes.

Chapter Seven - Pricing

As you're probably aware, there are more books, ideas, systems, and formulas for ''arriving'' at your book's perfect price point than there is tea in China.

Some pundits say : ''Go for .99 cents'' – because it's a low risk impluse buy. The assumption being that if the reader isn't over the moon with your book – he won't feel ripped off.

On the other hand, if your book rocks for the reader, you've created the expectation that the next book (assuming you'll be writing more than one) will be the same price. And if it's not – guess what ? That's right – he/she/it is going to cry ''rip-off !''

Other ''experts'' maintain you should price your book according to the value you place on it's content. The ''cream rises to the top'' assumption. However, success here depends on the cream rising before it curdles.

While the ''go with the flow'' school suggest you ''ballpark'' your opus with the ''average'' price in your genre.

What to do ? Be patient – I'll give you the answer shortly . But for now ? Just be aware of your price options :

.99 cents to 1.99 gives you a 35% royalty. Above that – 2.99 and above,you take home 70% of the retail selling price.

Chapter Eight

Basic Six – **KDP S**elect

Amazon's KDP Select program is a (Paternal?) Chokehold on your book, that prevents you from offering it for sale elsewhere for 90 days.

KDP's ''big carrot'' is the ability to offer your book for FREE for any five days in the three month period. The idea being that free downloads increase interest in, and attention to, your precious tome.

So, on one day one of your free promotion , you need to hit the ground running with the maximum promotional firepower you can muster.

Then, throughout the following four days, continue with a steady (but not over the top) stream of ads on smaller promo sites.

This will help to convince the big A that you're not just a one day wonder. And should have a positive impact on paid sales.

(NOTE : after the free period, you should be continuing the "slow promotional trickle" for a week or so BEFORE firing your massive "spiking the ranks" salvo.)

But if throwing your hat into the KDP ring does nothing for your bank balance, you're locked in for three big months..

Alternately – if you "just say no" to KDP, you have multiple sales channels available :

Apple (ibooks – stores in 51 countries)Barnes and Noble. Smashwords.(now distributing to a 400 store plus chain of English bookstores, among others) Nook. Oyster. Overdrive.(e-book platform serving over 20k libraries) Baker and Taylor. Flipkart. Scribd . Kobo. Etc.

Yes, it's "rock and a hard place" time again !

If you go with KDP – it's bye bye to all other book distribution possibilites for 90 days.

If you choose the big A – you gamble that those free downloads (plus the exceptional packaging/content of your claim to Literary fame and your ever so taseful promotions) will be worth being locked up in the Azon jail for three months.

As I said earlier, Amazon owns 60% of the book buying market, as of this writing.

And there is another, known, but underpublicized "Amazon advantage" (mentioned earlier) that is well worth considering. Once (and if) your book gains sufficient momentum Amazon will promote your book FOR FREE to it's best (prime) customers. They will even buy advertising on Google praising your creation.

Bottom line : "To KDP or not to KDP - that is the question." And only you, future big time Author, have the answer.

Chapter Nine – The Algo Dance

''Algorithm. '' You've doubtless heard the word before. Google has one. You tube has one. And, Amazon has one. It's the series of interdependent mathematically calculated events, that determine your books success or failure

Therefore, to maximize your chances of ''getting the Azon gold'' – you need to understand how the Azon Algo makes it's decisions.

Let me count the ways :

1. <u>Hourly.</u> Azon calculates the sales of all books and compares them against yours to arrive at a ''sales rank'' for all books. The LOWER your ranking – the greater your popularity, and (usually) the HIGHER your sales.

   So, a rank of 2000, is preferable to one of 20,000. <u>This free online tool</u> (not an affiliate link) will tell you how many sales a given book is getting.

2. <u>30 Day Average.</u> To arrive at their determination of your visibility, Azon divides your past 30 days sales with those of other books.

   The big take away with both of these metrics is that the big A wants to see (what it – the Algo -) considers a natural, ''organic'' increase in visibility/ popularity/sales.

   This translates as : ''Steady as she goes.'' Keep your book's fire (yes, it IS the most appropriate word) ''kindled'' not blazing.

<u>Best Practices Tip</u> : Keep your price to .99 cents during the (paid) launch period to maximize your cred with the 30 day average.

Chapter Ten

<u>You – The **B.T.A**. !</u>

HACK ATTACK !

"The time to look like a million bucks......is when you're green and wrinkled."
- Errol Flynn-

Someone who makes more money in a month than I do all year(Uber blogger John Chow) once wisely proclaimed : "In life perception is 50% of reality. On the internet,perception IS reality."

What does this have to do with your book ? Quite simply – if you LOOK like a BTA(Big Time Author) the World will accept that you are.

So – now that you've covered all the previous "looking like a BTA" bases with your incredible title, fantastic cover, riveting description, Great category choices, and laser focused keywords, it's time to add the "piece de la resistance" to your Author Image.

A paperback book. Published by CreateSpace. The other head of the Amazon hydra. You send them the same text you've used for kindle, the same cover, same book description....and they churn out a preview copy and snail mail it to you.

CreateSpace is a P.O.D. (print on demand) publisher. So, whenever you need a book(s) (for promotions, book signings) you place an order, pay a minimal price per book, and you're good to go.

There are two advantages to publishing with CreateSpace. The first is that you have another (potential source of income) Some folks prefer the touchy feely ambience of a paperback book. And (here's the biggie) they're willing to pay MORE for it ! Because (rightly or wrongly) paperback is considered "higher quality" than an e-book.

The second advantage is a MONSTEROUS one for your BTA image. IF you're willing to invest $10.

Here's why : If you publish with CreateSpace "normally" the publishing credit will go to them. Ie – "Published by CreateSpace."

But – and here's the deal breaker – if you pay $10 – you control the publishing credit !

This is HUGE ! - with a capital "H." As long as you don't do something like : "Joe's rinky dink dog training school publishing." (Sound like the publishing house of a BTA to you ?)

But – if you were to use a fictitious publishing name that was close enough to a real big time publishing co. - then book surfers would get the impression you really are (you guessed it) – a Big Time Author. Would they not ? (''Ransom House'' anyone?)

Chapter Eleven

<u>G</u>old, <u>B</u>rass, <u>I</u>ron or <u>S</u>quirrel <u>D</u>ookie

Those are basically the four possible ratings when someone reviews your book. (Although they might instead use a combination/lack of stars to express their opinion)

Reviews are the one thing (actually probably the only thing) that ''Kindle Consellors '' agree on. You absolutely, positively, no way around it, need reviews. (The old ''social proof'' rant. Or as I like to call it ''Social Sheep'')

So – like it or not – you have to deal with it.

Understand that there are two kinds of reviews : The ''I bought your book and here's what I think of it '' kind, and ''Editorial Reviews '' ie – newspapers, trade publications, other (preferably well known) authors, and/or media gurus.

You've doubtless hear a zillion times that the ''best'' way to get the former type of reviews is to ask family and friends. Or contact all the Amazon ''top 100 reviewers.'' (Good luck on that one.)

While those are do-able strategies to get the six minimum reviews you need to get the book ball rolling (I'll explain why six shortly) – they obviously do NOTHING for sales velocity. Which is what Azon salivates over.

You may have seen some reviews which began with : '' I was given this book in exchange for an honest review. ''

Amazon has now nuked all of those reviews. So – not an option. And, frankly, good riddance . All they screamed was : ''DESPERATION ! ''

You've heard, undoubtedly, that some unscrupulous Authors-to-be pay people from freelance internet sites to buy their book and leave a review. (In most cases, one supplied by the wannabe Author.)

Guess what – the big A has heard about this too. LLLLLong ago. And they regularly mount sting operations to catch the culprits.

Not a good investment for any Author. Particular one with a BTA presence. Wouldn't you agree ?

How many reviews do you need ? Six for Need. The skies the limit for the number of reviews you'd like.

Why Six? Here's the reason : The majority of surfers who have been sufficiently dazzled by your presentation to make it this far, are, in the majority of cases, only going to read the first three reviews. (If that.) The ones Amazon displays in full to the left of the sales page.

If these reviews echo your U.S.P, confidence/interest increased, that surfer will head straight to your 10% preview. And hopefully do the "buy with one click" dance.

These first three full reviews are, hands down the most important. Because the big A cuts off the next three reviews, which appear as headlines and short paragraph page right.

After "verified Amazon purchase" and the star rating, you get something like : "I thought this book was going to be another cliche how to...but i was happily suprised to discover...."

Bottom Line : The majority of surfers won't bother with these truncated reviews, but for the minority that do, they've "got your back."

Best Practices Note : Amazon expects that you WILL ask your family and friends to review. After all, it IS reasonable. However, this is sort of a"Clinton-ism" (ie- "Don't ask – don't tell") So, don't have any reviews that share your last name. Or are obviously an Aunt or Uncle gushing praise over their favorite Nephew/Niece.

An automated review solution I recommend (NOT an affiliate link) is Deb Drums - Book Reviewer Targeter. (http://debdrum.com)

Herself an Author, Deb created this tool originally for her own use. As she was experiencing exactly the same "review challenges" that all Authors who aren't (yet) on the NY Times best seller chart face.

Editorial Reviews are, at first glance, a harder nut to crack. But, as you might imagine, I DO have a "work-around" (coming up soon)

But first, let's be clear on the nature of the beast. An Editorial Review is considered to be an independant, unbiased, verifiable testament of your towering talent.

If you can get one(and you can, as you'll learn shortly) you should include it in your listing BEFORE you publish.

So you can hit the ground with it, and (asap thereafter, like 24 hours) 6 verified paid positive reviews. Maximum firepower !

There are two ways to score an Editorial review (Unless you happen to have a relative high up at a major newspaper, or drink at the same bar as a famous Author/Media Guru,)

The first is the obvious. You pay for one. The big man on campus in the paid reviews game is 'Kirkus Reviews." For $425, they'll give you 300 words (approx) of neutral to effusive comment. And, if you want it even faster – like in 4 to 6 weeks – you'll need to pay $525. If, for whatever reason they choose not to review , they'll send your cash back .

Considering Kirkus is a "pay for play" outfit – I can't begin to understand why they're considered "prestigious." But hey – shit happens – as they say in San Diego.

If you're unlucky enough not to have a major newspaper reviewer in your pocket and all you have for Kirkus et al, is a bronx cheer ,- no worries – there is a FREE option.

However, it is against Amazon's Terms of Service. That said, it is a common and long used technique. (Like the "Don't ask – don't tell" of family/friends reviews) It can, and has, helped many first time Authors on a limited/non-existent budget create the initial "social proof " necessary to attract potential readers.

DISCLAIMER : *I'm not suggesting/proposing that you use this technique. It's provided solely for your information. You do with it what you will.*

Here's how it works : You sign up for a free blog on the internet. You give it a (to you) "prestigious/review style" name. ("Kirk's Reviews ?", "New and Book-Worthy ?")

Then you (writing in an atypical voice) or a literate friend following your instructions, write the review. (Hint : this is a GOLDEN chance to include some of the marvy keywords that didn't make it into your 7 keyword quota.)

Obviously, the "reviewer" should have a trendy and/or pompous pen name. (But don't go overboard. The goal is reality. Not comedy.)

Once you've proofed the review – hit that publish button ! Allllllllrighty then ! Your praises are now being sung to all the Wired World.

Now copy that blog review into your book pages "Editorial Review" section, with, of course the appropriate credit at the bottom. (html is not allowed in the Editorial Review)
If your review is balanced and well written, it will be accepted without question by the majority of surfers.

The anal rententive nit picking never cracked a smile minority will paste the blog name in their browsers..and discover to their disappointment that.....Drat !..it is REAL !

Chapter Twelve

Surfin' the Ama-Zone

Remember I said I'd tell you how to price your book ? Well - grab a quick coffee – because we're almost there.

But first – let me explain WHY. It's all to do with what Amazon calls : "Sales Velocity." In other words – how many sales your book has in a given time span. (The shorter the better.)

Sales Velocity is more important than reviews. Reviews supply the social proof to (hopefully) persuade surfers to "look inside" and (again, hopefully,) " buy with one click"

But Sales Velocity says to Amazon : "Hey...this thing is really taking off....so I guess we should give it a little push......"

So, as an Author (and entrepeneur) your job is to simultaneously "enable " reviews and sales. Much easier than you'd imagine.

Since you already know how to handle reviews, it's time to concentrate on sales.

We'll do this indirectly. Because, unless you have a personal posse of 50 to 100 friends with credit cards poised to ''pump up'' your sales ballon – this is the next best way.

And it leverages the ''KDP Select stranglehold.'' Here's how it works :

First, get on board the KDP train and make your book free for two days. Two to Three weeks in the future.

Then go to the PAID book promotion sites and create an ad that concludes with the dates of your freebie.

Since you ARE a B.T.A. ,in your mind, and want to be, in the minds of others, your ad should obviously be ''B.T.A. Quality.'' Stylish fonts , Graphically compelling. Great colors. Irresistible call to action. (The ''C.T.A.'') ie – ''Free one day only – then $4.99''

If a surfer has even a moderate interest in your subject/niche, that price point, coupled with your B.T.A. Image, will have them thinking : ''The inside scoop on Underwater Welding for Free instead of $4.99 ?...definitely gonna make a note to grab that ! '' (p.s. ''underwater welding '' is a *real* niche.)

Naturally, your book cover should figure prominently here, as it's the visual ''branding'' that will trigger the surfer's memory when they click through to Amazon.

Even if you have some graphic/design/advertising ability, you'd be shooting yourself in the foot not to invest some time looking at the real B.T.A.'s ad's on these sites. And noting the design elements that catch YOUR eye.

As they most certainly will do the same for other eyeballs . Wouldn't you agree ?

On the other side of the coin, if you can't draw a straight line even with a ruler – get professional help. And cool your jets. It won't cost an arm and a leg. There are many graphic smarties who can give you a big visual leg up for less than the cost of a nice dinner for two. (With wine, of course!) Again – don't skip my resources section.

*You should price the CreateSpace version of your book between $10.99 and $12.99 (just like REAL B.T.A.'s do!)

Chapter Thirteen

A Huge Nugget

HACK ATTACK !

While sales are not unimportant to the big A – they place as much (or more) weight on "conversions." That is – the process that converts a surfer into a buyer.

This is why you DO NOT want to send buyers DIRECTLY to your book listing. Send them to the first page of the genre your opus is in. Instruct them to go through each page until they finally(huff huff, puff puff) arrive at your listing. (Probably at the bottom of page three – if you're lucky.) THEN – click and buy.

When Amazon sees this (and they track EVERYTHING (" every move you make, every breath you take" etc.) the big A says : "Wow...that surfer went through all three pages to get to this book...so it must really be trending......we should definitely give this a push !"

Chapter Fourteen

Searching for Eyeballs

That's what book promotion really comes down to. I'm sure you've heard the old adage : "Publish or Perish. ?" Well, if you publish and don't promote, you absolutely WILL perish ! (Unless you've been sprinkled with Amanda Hocking fairy dust.)

There are various methods for attracting those eyeballs, paid and free. But obviously paid will give you the best (pun intended) "bang for your buck."

The paid options include, but are not limited to, the following :

Book Review sites. (other than "Book Bub.")

"Solo ads" Solo Ads are your ad broadcast to the email list of someone with an email list of prospective readers in your genre. You pay them, usually,by the click to your opt-in page .

Twitter. (a word of caution here : Buy directly from twitter. Buying a ''spot'' on the account of someone with gazillions of followers, is like putting your plumbing service listing in the white pages and hoping that people with leaky taps will find you.) Keep in mind, the life of a tweet is fifteen seconds.

Pinterest. As of this writing, Pinterest generates more traffic than Twitter and Facebook combined.

Facebook. The advantage of facebook ads is that you can specifically target people who have read other author's books. So – if your magnum opus is in the same/similar genre...you could get some traction.

You Tube Video Ads. Have all (and more) precision targeting metrics than Facebook, and, as of this writing, are *insanely* inexpensive.

Instagram. As you've probably heard generates more traffic than virtually all of it's social media competitors combined. That's the good news. The bad – is that the median age of ''instanaughts '' is 25. So – unless you (or your promotional posse) have the time and energy to post multiple images,memes and hashtags daily to promote your gaming or entertainment oriented tome - I'd give Instagram a pass.

BookBub. Is the ''800 lb. Gorilla'' of paid book promotion. You submit your book for review. If they give it a ''thumbs up'', then they'll *let you* pay serious bucks to blast it out to their massive ''customers-who-love-books-like-yours-list.''

You've also heard that Authors should have an extensive ''social media presence. '' Right ?

Author web site .Facebook fan page . G plus page. Twitter account. Pinterest, yada, yada, yada. Absolutely essential – *if you're an established Author* !
Otherwise you're peeing into the wind.

Wth two exceptions :

1. **Author website**. Because : a) It's free. (Wordpress.com, Blogger.com, etc) b) it enables you to collect email addresses (from those facebook, solo, and other ads, via an ''opt-in '' form. Enabling you to begin to create a rapport with that list. Which, done correctly, will ultimately lead to sales. This is ''List Building.'' We'll dive into it shortly.

2. **Facebook Fan Page**. Also free to create. Send opt-ins from your facebook ads here, to like and share your preview book snippets. Run contests and giveaways. Create an "early readers" group. To get feedback. Offer your early readers a bonus (free book/report/someone else wonderful) for that feedback.

   You'll find that the majority, will, without further prompting, buy the book when it's published. But just selling your book, suprise,suprise, is not the end goal. The end goal, The "Holy Grail" of book (and all marketing) is...

BUILDING A LIST !

A list of people who have expressed a serious interest in you. And the value you offer. In this case – through your books.

If your literary goals are, as I assume – "Long Term" – You must absolutely, positively no if ands or buts, no excuses allowed – _BUILD A LIST_ !"

Because then YOU not Amazon, not anyone else, controls YOUR business.

When you have a new book – You mail your list. When you need reviews – You mail your list. When you want feedback on future book topics – You mail your list.

The takeaway here, folks, is : _INDEPENDANCE_. In big , glowing Neon letters. Sound good to you ?

Free Book Promotion :

Obviously – when your book is live – there are a multitude of Free Book sites on the internet. I'm not going to rattle off the too long list here – as these sites come and go. Just Google "free book sites" when you're ready.

Perhaps not as immediately logical – but much mo' beddah' is to have "Influencers" share your book – before it's published.

So..who are "influencers ?" Uh.....they would be....uh..people with..."influence ?" Would they not, ? People with Authority, fans, and most probably a gigantic email list ? People like REAL Big Time Authors, Social Media gurus, Uber famous bloggers. Getting my drift ?

So how do you – B.T.A in waiting, connect with this upper echelon of intensive influence ?

Let us count the ways :

1. <u>You send them a simple no frills, recorded in your kitchen video</u>. Of you, sincerely, honestly and briefly (like less than 90 seconds) telling them what the connection is between your book and what they do – and why they should care.

"But I have a face made for radio ! " is NOT an excuse. It is an ADVANTAGE – because they will definitely pay attention. (And hey, most everyone has a "radio face" – so don't go thinkin' you're special – ok ?)

"But I don't have a video camera, or proper lights, etc" – This is the LAMEST of excuses ! Every computer these days comes with a WEBCAM.

2. <u>You research them.</u> As if they were the subject of your next book. Their education. Likes/dislikes. Achievements . Associates. Are they on Linkedin ? Who do you know that might know anyone in their organization/club, etc. Reverse engineer. Start with your desired end result, then work backward. And when you get that golden contact : *Send them your video*. Email ain't gonna cut it. (But then – you knew that already – right?)

HACK ATTACK !

Here are two more FREE techniques that, while not guaranteed to help – will absolutely not hurt. The first is generally referred to as the "Authority Piggyback." Because you will be associating yourself with ("piggybacking") the Authority of an established Author.

Here's how it works : Select the best selling book in your genre, or the book, for whatever reason you want to be associated with. Then, because you are a fellow Amazon Author, you have the ability to review any book on the big A.

You sign in where Azon invites you to "leave a review", and you'll be whisked to the appropriate form.

You should start your review by mentioning YOUR BOOK in the first sentence. Because (And here's where the "no Amanda Hocking fairy dust" magic needed comes in) Mr. Bezos and Co. Will give you a LIVE LINK directly to your book.

So, your first sentence should go something like : "As the Author of <u>War and Peas. </u>I know a thing or two about..."

Azon will cut the rest of your review off after the first few sentences. That's why you want to get your title/link in asap.

While it doesn't have to be long, your review should, of course, contribute value, and give the impression you are an Author of the same stature. (More BTA dust!)

Remember I said there was an exception to the reality : "Readers search for books where books are sold ?" Well – this is it :

The second FREE (and potentially valuable if finessed correctly) technique is : GOODREADS. The, for want of a better description, "internet book club" with 40 million readers owned by......you guessed it......Amazon.

Free to join . Overflowing with free and paid promotional opportunities.

Your own Author profile, Bio.Bond with readers, other Authors, create contests, book giveaways, get reviews, upload sample chapters, *SCHMOOZE* !

Bottom line : It's Amazon, and it's free. And, hey guess what – all the big time Authors use it. So – now, that means you . Right ?

Chapter Fifteen

<u>Hey Mom – Look at Me</u> !

One aspect of paid promotion that is a large (and very expensive) "Don't go there" are Book Trailers. Mini-videos "showcasing" the Author, his deep thoughts, his home, his animals.

The sales pitch here is that this "creates rapport" and "bonds" the Author with the reader/prospective reader. This is elephant do-do.

What it creates are large paydays for the video producers.

But wait you say...all the big Authors have them.....if I'm trying to establish a BTA image, shouldn't I have one too ?

The answer is : If it strokes your ego, and you have the money – go for it. But don't expect a tsunami of sales as a result.

Yes, the real Big Time Authors have them, because :

A) Their publishers pay for it. (And use it in all their media advertising.)

B) Their ESTABLISHED stature (ie – multiple mega books) means that ''the reading public'' is dying to know where their ideas come from, what they eat for breakfast, and if they dye their hair.

They could give a rat's ass about you. Because, despite your BTA image, at this point, you are un-established.

Bottom Line : Book Trailers are 100% vanity. Zero R.O.I. for the un-established.

Chapter Sixteen

More **M**oney ! With (almost) **N**o **M**ore **W**ork.

Cool your jets ! I'm not morphing into a hype-heavy Internet marketer. But, amazing as it seems, that ''too good to be true'' title, really is true.

But wait – there's more ! The two money makers I'm about to hip you to, will also promote your book !

Money maker number one : An audio version of your book. (preferably read by you – not some ''expert narrator.'' (Who would cost you both arms and legs) As you may know, although they've been around for awhile, audio books are enjoying a – dare I say – resurgence. Largely due to modern mobile lifestyles.

Folks are always on the move these days. And so, entertainment/information they can listen to while driving or doing yard work is the order of the day.

You've already written your book. (that's the "no more work " part.) All you need to do now is record it. A $50 microphone and free recording software from the internet are all you need to create the listenable version of your written masterpiece.

OK – so you record your book. Now what ? How do you distribute it to your (soon to be) legions of fans ? Luckily, the big A, once again, has "got your back."

They have a sister company which, wait for it – *distributes audio books.* It's called : "ACX. " (a clever acyronym for "Audio Creation Exchange") As long as your recording quality is up to snuff (and they'll advise you before you rev up your vocal cords) ACX will distribute your literary claim to fame to Amazon, itunes, and "Audible." (the evil twin of ACX)

There's no upfront cost to ACX, as they, like Amazon take a few small nuggets from your royalty gold.

So, with one swell foop, you have increased possibilities for revenue and promotion. (Can you say : "Win – Win ?")

(NOTE : There are companies known as : "Audio Aggregators" who will distribute your vocal performance to a variety of locations other than those covered by Audible.)

Money Maker Number two : Podcasts. Hey – you already have the finished audio. All you need to do now is exchange your chapter titles for "episode" ones.

 So , if your audio book has 20 chapters – viola ! - you have 20 podcast episodes. More than enough to get you rolling.

There are expenses here. But they're not monumental. Like a website, a podcast must be "hosted" somewhere. That is : Your episodes will live at a central location online. And when folks click a link(on itunes or other sales location) your "host" will "serve" them your podcast.

Podcast Hosting (as of this writing) is around $30@month. And there are several providers.

HOT TIP : itunes is the big man on the podcasting campus. And like the big A, will promote you on their own steam, if they see a "flurry" of initial interest. The general consensus is that "flurry" is a minimum of 12 subscribers in the first 24 to 48 hours. (Obviously the sooner the better)

You do have at least 12 friends, don't you ?

While itunes is the ''800 lb gorilla'' of podcasting, there are several lesser primates that shouldn't be overlooked. (Hint : Google ''Podcast Hosts'')

Chapter Seventeen

<u>M</u>odelling.

Not to sound like Dirty Harry here but, ''The question you gotta ask yourself is..do you want to be an Entrepeneur ? Or an Author?......wannabe !!!???

Entrepeneurs look at what's selling at any given moment, then '' modelling '' the success/topic of that Author, create a similar book.

So – if ''Underwater fitness for Women over 50'' is the trendy topic , you can expect : '' 25 hacks for Women over 50 to improve their Underwater Fitness Training.'', ''The Unoffical Underwater Fitness for Women over 50 Progress Journal, etc, etc.

You're getting my drift, are you not?

OK, technically, if you write a book, you're an Author. And, if that book sells, viola, you've morphed into a paid Author. The entrepeneur kind. Nothing wrong with that.

IF your end goal is simply collecting pictures of dead presidents. And you can collect a lot of them with this method.

But what you can't do with the entrepeneur approach is build a loyal fan base who love your work and(here's the takeaway) will buy from you every time you have a new book/DVD/Event, or monogrammed chef's apron.

There's an old marketing joke that completely describes the modelling entrepeneur M.O.

Question : '' What does the top salesman in the World do next year ?
Answer : ''He does it all over again.''

My point here is that modelling rarely produces long haul Authors. And/or Blockbusters.

Who did E.L. James ''model'' for her obscenely (pun intended) successful ''5O

Shades" series ? (You'll notice, and I hope appreciate, I resisted the enormous temptation to comment on the quality of her writing)

I'm assuming you're a writer who wants to be an Author. A paid one . Who's "in it" for the long haul.

Please, don't prove me wrong.

Chapter Eighteen

Bonus Chapter – from Amy Harrop, Author, Teacher, Content Creator.

How to Grow Your Audience with Permafree Content

One of the best ways to leverage the huge audience that is on Amazon Kindle and other book platforms is to offer a book as permafree. Permafree means permanently free and it is not something that Amazon actively encourages or promotes in their Kindle publishing program. They would much rather you use KDP select, where you can offer your book for free up to five days every 90 days, and continually free for KDP select members only.

However, permafree books can be a great way to sell your paid content, gain massive exposure, and win over new readers. Whether you are a non-fiction or a fiction author, having at least one title that is permafree will help you continually attract new readers.

For example, my permafree book, **Leave The Job Behind** became a #1 bestseller in the Self Help-Short Reads category for free books, and has had over 1000 downloads since publication.

In this chapter I'm going to share with you the fastest and easiest strategies for making your content, permafree on Kindle and other popular book venues despite the fact that Amazon does not allow you to list your book directly for free.

Why Is Permafree An Effective Publishing Strategy?
Why does permafree work so well for authors? A few reasons:
- Giving somebody something for free triggers the law of reciprocity. In terms of publishing, if people check out your free book, and they like it, there is a very good chance they will follow up and take further action, such as checking out your other paid books, signing up to your email newsletter, and following you

on social media- *especially if you ask them to.*

- You can build a relationship with people who otherwise may not have discovered your content. In today's crowded publishing marketplace, it can be difficult for your book to found by digital browsers.

- It allows you to leverage what I like to call *other people's audiences*. Whether that is on Amazon's Kindle platform, the iBookstore, Barnes & Noble, or other book platforms, allows you to gain exposure to massive amounts of people quickly and easily.

Creating a Permafree Book

Before you go through the actual steps of publishing a permafree book, you should give some thought as to what type of book you want to publish.

Fiction

If you are publishing fiction, one of the best types of content to permafree publish is the first book in a series. That way, you provide the opportunity for people to get introduced to your fictional world, and to continue reading the second, paid book in the series. This is something to seriously consider, because series' tend to do better than stand-alone books overall.

Non-Fiction

For non-fiction content, you should keep your book very focused. For example, books that specifically address one problem or course of action.

Publishing Considerations

- **Length**. Short, but not too short. You want content that people can easily consume and not leave collecting dust. It should feel long enough where the person feels they are getting good value, even if they didn't pay for it, which will encourage them to want to check out your paid content.

- **Next Steps.** Make sure you have opportunities built into your book for people to take action. You may have additional books they can purchase. They can sign up for your email newsletter inside the book, or even better, you give away something free as an incentive for them to sign up. This does require that you have an email service, but it's been well documented that authors who have responsive email lists are able to sell books faster it easier.

- **Title, description, and cover**- These are also incredibly important, even if you are publishing free content. You want to have a compelling title and description that motivates someone to take the next step of downloading your book. In addition, you want to have a professional looking cover. Just because your book is free doesn't mean it should look cheap.

Publishing Your Permafree Book

Now that you have your content, it's time to publish your book. You cannot publish a book as free directly to Amazon's Kindle. First of all, Amazon does not want the market flooded with massive amounts of free books. Secondly, they really want authors and publishers to use their KDP select exclusive program.

But with the permafree model your book can be free on not only Kindle, but other e-book platforms, so you can get as wide as an audience exposure as possible.

Here is a step-by-step guide to publishing permafree:

1. Publish your book to Amazon Kindle for $.99. Do not enroll it in the KDP Select program. Also, pay special attention to the categories that you select for your book. It's better to try to put your book and categories that are smaller and don't have as many books published in. That will make it easier for you to actually have your book be on the bestseller list, which will give your book even more exposure.

2. Once your book is published on Amazon, head over to http://Draft2Digital.com and publish your book there. D2D is a publishing aggregator and will publish your book to multiple platforms (like iBookstore, Barnes & Noble, etc.) at once. D2D is similar to Smashwords, but I think it's much easier to use. They will publish your book to multiple platforms, and take a small percentage of your royalties. You can learn more about publishing your book through D2D here: http://Draft2Digital.com When you publish, make sure you price your book at $0.00, which is allowed through D2D.

3. Once your book is live, D2D will let you know when it's been successfully published to whatever platforms you selected. You may have to wait a few days. Navigate directly to the platforms and find the links where your book is live. You want to have a specific link showing your book is free. These would be places like Barnes & Noble, Kobo, and the iBookstore. You can get most of

the links inside your D2D account. Collect at least three links of stores where your book is free. Next, go inside your KDP dashboard, and contact Amazon's KDP customer service. **Let them know that you have found your book for free on other platforms, and put the links to these other platforms inside your email so they can see them.** Do not just link to D2D, you must link to the specific stores.

Tell KDP that you would appreciate it if they would price match your book on Kindle as well. Most likely they will get back to you and let you know they'll take a look, and then they will change your book to free. They may not let you know they changed it to free, you just have to check periodically, but it shouldn't take more than a few days or so. If you don't hear back, write them again, I would suggest opening up a new ticket with them so you can reach somebody else there.

Voilà, your book is now free on massive platforms!

Promoting Your Permafree Book

Once your book is published, it's a good idea to give your book a kick start in terms of exposure. You can do this first by getting some reviews, and then promoting your free book.

Getting reviews: this is often the most difficult part when you're publishing. If you have any type of following or email list, this is a great source for some initial reviews. Simply let them know your book is free and you would appreciate some reviews. A few other ways are:

- Run a promotion through http://librarything.com. You have to sign up as a member, but you can do by reading other books or paying a very small membership fee. Once you do that, you can run book promotions for e-books and giveaway up to 100 copies for free.

- You can also find similar books in your niche on Amazon and look at the reviewers. Many reviewers will have contact information in their Amazon profile. If they do, you can let them know that you have a similar book to one they reviewed for free and ask if they'd like to check it out and leave you or review. This is very tedious and time-consuming, and you might want to consider outsourcing this manual task on something like Fiverr.

Once you've had 3 to 5 reviews, you can promote your free book with some of the e-book listing services. While you can get a lot of exposure with paid ads, if your book is free and you're just getting started, you may want to just submit to the free places first. Here is a good list of places to submit your book:

http://www.trainingauthors.com/47-places-to-submit-your-free-kdp-promotion-for-your-kindle-ebook/

If you've chosen your category wisely, once people start downloading your free book it will be relatively easy for your book to end up on the free bestseller charts. This will continue to give your book more exposure and more readers.
Publishing a few permafree books is a great way to increase your exposure as an author, whether you're a fiction or nonfiction writer. Permafree allows you to establish authority, get the word out about your content to new readers, and build a dedicated tribe who cannot wait to read your next book.

About Amy Harrop
Amy Harrop is a writer, teacher, and content creator specializing in helping people create passive content income streams. Visit http://AmyHarrop.com and grab her FREE report- *Three Fast Fixes For Your Book*

A Big "Thank You" to Amy for that informative and <u>*actionable*</u> chapter !

But wait – There's more !

Chapter Nineteen

Yes, ole' Tom is going to continue to overdeliver big time, with ANOTHER Bonus chapter.

Ths one from Best Selling Amazon Author Derek Doepker. He's written more than seven books in various genres. Most noteably, "Breakthrough Your B.S." and "Why Authors Fail." Two books to definitely check out definitely check out !

Derek is also the main man behind ebookbestsellersecrets.com, and excuseproof.com. And, like me, he regards self-publishing as equal parts creativity and business smarts.

Listen up. This guy has the goods.

7 Key Principles Ever Author Needs To Know

1. People aren't buying WHAT you say, they're buying HOW you say it.

Having the same information delivered in a different voice or style is not the same experience. #NoDuh

As a self-help author, I can't really come up with a "new" way to improve someone's life. What I can do is *deliver the message* in a new way. I can deliver the message in a style that's entertaining instead of boring. I can use parables and stories to teach instead of shoving down people's throats a bunch of "do this, don't do that" commands. I can use my personality to resonate with particular readers who might not listen to other authors.

What is your voice? Style? Personality? Unique system or methodology?

Fiction authors are included in this. All fiction stories are essentially the Hero's Journey. All romantic comedies and paranormal thrillers and whatever other genre all follow a similar set of themes. Yet they're all different experiences based on the style of the author.

Finally, this is just as important to remember if you have books ghostwritten. Your brand and packaging is your style. "History In A Hurry" is a made-up brand I just came up with for people that want historical topics delivered in easily digestible chunks.

If you write a lukewarm "me too" book that's packaged like all the other books on the topic, you're not going to make it (unless you're lucky) long-term in the book publishing world.

I didn't start with a style other than my own voice, and that's enough. It will evolve over time. You can't *sit around* trying to find your voice. Discovering your unique style requires putting writing out there, getting feedback, failing, and making adjustments over time.

If you can't make your book stand out, it will get lost in a sea of competing books. #RealTalk

2. There's no "safe" way to make a breakthrough.

If you want to have massive success, this requires being a trailblazer on some level. You can study and model others, but the biggest companies and authors had to discover, through trial, error, failures, and setbacks their own personal path to success.

A setback can be a setup for success – if you get feedback and lessons from the experience.

Failure becomes feedback, and feedback is the foundation for FUTURE success.

Failure + Feedback = Future Success

The more willing you are to fail compared to your competition, the more of a competitive edge you'll have.

Learn what you can from my trainings and other trainings...

But maintain a good ratio of studying proven strategies + trying things out and seeing what works.

Spend too much time in either side, and you'll either get stuck in paralysis by analysis or spinning your wheels going nowhere.

3. You are a farmer. You can't make plants grow, but you can plant seeds in the right environment.

You, as in just what you do by yourself, can only get the word out to so many people about your books. Amazon (or other retailers), your fans, and the platforms of other influencers will be largely responsible for selling your books.

The real quality questions include how do I sell my readers on promoting my book for me?

How do I sell influencers on reading my book and sharing it?

This is largely what this training is about. You can't sell effectively by being pushy, but rather by "pulling" people in with captivating hooks and intrigue.

4. If you only focus on one method to sell your own books...

Build. Your. List.

That's it.

Build an email list of engaged followers.

Connect with me if you want details for something that may help with this. This guide will show you giveaways and other methods I've used of doing this.

If you're going to spend your time doing one thing on your own, it's this.

Now I will add a caveat...

"Build a list" is a WHAT to do thing.

The "how to THINK" thing is thinking like a salesperson and using the skills of influence.

A big email list won't do jack if you send them things they don't want.

You need to know how to sell, and this will serve you in many ways.

In fact, if you can REALLY sell, you could technically never build your own list (not recommended) because you can persuade and negotiate deals with other people's lists to sell your books for you.

In actuality, you'll want to do both.

The #1 thing to REALLY do to sell more books is improving your influence and people skills.

Note: I'm reading the book Switch by Jack Schafer and find it valuable for these types of skills. The books Influence by Robert Cialdini and Yes! are also recommended as well.

5. Often full time authors write many books or...

With a few exceptions, many authors who make their living self-publishing are consistently pumping out books. This is one model.

If you don't want to do this, you need to still be pumping out podcast interviews (Hal Elrod claimed this helped him), valuable content and training courses, speaking, blogging, or doing something to get exposure on an on-going basis. You might get lucky and have a single book become a runaway hit that sets you for life, but don't bank on it.

I'm not able to consistently drive sales to my books without regular promotions. This means even I have to go back to the drawing board and recommit to building my email list, doing more interviews, putting out more videos, and hustling to make things happen in 2016.

Take home point... **always be marketing** yourself and your work. Thanks to James Malinchak for the always be marketing concept.

6. Understand the slingshot.

How do you make a muscle stronger?

You make it weaker…

Temporarily.

Ever think about that? You literally make your muscles weaker by doing resistance training and only days later do they ever become stronger.

This is what I call the slingshot effect. Go in the OPPOSITE direction of what you want, and it can release to go towards what you do want.

If you go after what you want right away, such as a book sale, you might not get it.

But if you're willing to forego a short-term book sale to say, give away a free copy to a die-hard fan, then weeks later they might tell all their friends about it who go out and read it.

I will invest in Amazon's advertising platform. Does it show a profit? No… but I'll take a short-term loss for a long-term gain.

During a book's launch, I'll invest $10 in advertising even if I only make an extra 5 sales a day at .99 cents (35 cents per book sale for $1 a day in royalties).

Why?

Because those 5 sales a day might be just enough to keep me ranking higher in the bestsellers list.

The higher ranking leads to more organic sales at .99 cents thereby leading to more sales than just those 5 sales.

The more organic sales leads to more potential readers of my OTHER books at regular price ultimately almost breaking even.

In the long-term, with enough future books and exposure, this can turn a profit.

Don't worry if you don't understand Amazon's algorithm right now. The take home point is that it's worth taking a loss upfront in order to have a bigger gain down the road.

Another thing to consider is this…

How you want to finish isn't the same way you need to start.

You might want a bestselling book…

But your first book might not be that bestselling book. So what?

If it takes getting a few books out there to get your feet wet, learn the ins and outs, and build your tribe, and these are all pieces to make say your fourth book a bestseller…

Isn't it worth it?

Don't people spend tens of thousands of dollars and years of their life to get a college education?

Isn't one or two measly years and maybe a few hundred or few thousand dollars a pretty small investment to become a bestselling author?

Don't many people sacrifice *ten times* that much to get a college degree and ultimately end up with a crappy job they don't even want?

I'm amazed at the fear people have of "failing" in self-publishing or business.

9/10 businesses fail. So. Freakin. What?

Does that mean don't start a business? Does that mean get stuck in paralysis by analysis trying to be the exception to the trend? NEITHER of these approaches work.

Learn from successful businesses to minimize the risk, but be willing to fail nine times because the 10th time that's a success can bring in so much money and freedom that it makes up for the nine failures. The one business that does make it can earn more in a couple years than some make in a lifetime of a "safe" job.

Would you rather have a few years of failure and then live the rest of your life doing what you love or settle for mediocrity and spend the rest of your life in regret?

7. Focus on giving, and be willing to ask.

Give value. The ASK for, rather than demand for, things in return.

Need help with something?

Ask, "How can I _give_ help?"

Do this enough, and when you need a favor…

Strangely enough you might seem to get it.

Give a tremendously valuable book to the world, and people will often share it, especially when you ask.

Give a curiosity inducing "hook" to an influencer, and they'll often be willing to check it out, especially when you ask.

Give free content to people just for the hell of it, and they'll often be willing to buy stuff, especially when you ask.

I know this sounds stupid obvious, but I highly suggest you stop and consider how often you're asking "How can I get (book sales, exposure, more reviews)?" instead of "How can I GIVE value?"

If the ratio is skewed too much in favor of trying to get things, then this may be why (going back to the slingshot) you're not getting it.

Derek Doepker is founder of EbookBestsellerSecrets.com and author of the #1 bestselling book Why Authors Fail.

Chapter 20

Good Bye ? Or just Au Revoir ?

OK – that's (almost)it !

Along with those two Nugget packed contributions from Derek and Amy, I've just given you the benefit of my REAL LIFE experience (so far)as a Literary Agent, Book Doctor and Publisher. In the shortest, most complete, nugget filled, no fluff way I know..

If you implement the blueprint I've laid out – you absolutely *will* enhance your possibilities of entering the golden circle of Writers(at all levels) who become Authors. The Paid kind.

As complete as the preceding has been, if you're stoked to go even deeper, you have two options :

1. **Personal Email Coaching**.

Although my private coaching program remains closed, in order to help as many writers as possible become (paid) Authors, I'm offering limited personal email consultations – ONLY to buyers of this book.

("Personal" meaning I , and only I will be replying to you – not one of my staff !)

Cleverly titled : **"Talk to Tom."** You may ask me any and all questions relating to self-publishing. 5 questions @week for one month. (ie – 20 questions @month) (NOTE : *I will not review manuscripts.*)

The fee is $127. And I'm only accepting 20 applicants. To ensure I can give you my best.

If you see the value here – shoot me a mail at : firstclass.artists@gmail.com, with "TTT" in the subject line, and we'll get you hooked up.

2. **My Udemy Course** – http://udemy.com/self-publishing-success-kindle-and-beyond can help take your game to the next level.

If you enjoyed this book, by leaving a short review, you'll help others receive the benefit you've just enjoyed. And your comments will help me improve so that I may serve you better.

I wish you the greatest possible success in Literature and Life, and look forward to hearing your self publishing success story !

Warmest Regards,

Tom.

www.ingramcontent.com/pod-product-compliance
Lightning Source LLC
Chambersburg PA
CBHW081310180526
45170CB00007B/2650